MINI MAKERS

by Rebecca Felix and
Ruthie Van Oosbree

CAPSTONE PRESS
a capstone imprint

Dabble Lab is published by Capstone Press, an imprint of Capstone.
1710 Roe Crest Drive, North Mankato, Minnesota 56003
capstonepub.com

Copyright © 2024 by Capstone. All rights reserved. No part of this publication may be reproduced in whole or in part, or stored in a retrieval system, or transmitted in any form or by any means, electronic, mechanical, photocopying, recording, or otherwise, without written permission of the publisher.

Library of Congress Cataloging-in-Publication Data
Names: Felix, Rebecca, 1984- author. | Van Oosbree, Ruthie, author.
Title: Mini origami to fold with flair / by Rebecca Felix and Ruthie Van Oosbree.
Description: North Mankato, Minnesota : Capstone Press, a Capstone imprint, [2024] | Series: Mini makers | Includes bibliographical references. | Audience: Ages 8 to 11 | Audience: Grades 4-6 | Summary: "Looking to learn the art of origami? Think mini! Fold a pretty, bitty butterfly. Create a super-small pot to hold tiny paper plants. Craft a cute crown fit for a king or queen. Then display your mini masterpieces for everyone to see. Easy instructions and step-by-step photos will help you become a miniature master. Tiny origami is tons of fun!"— Provided by publisher.
Identifiers: LCCN 2022051636 (print) | LCCN 2022051637 (ebook) | ISBN 9781669016717 (hardcover) | ISBN 9781669016687 (pdf) | ISBN 9781669016700 (kindle edition) | ISBN 9781669016540 (epub)
Subjects: LCSH: Origami—Juvenile literature. | Miniature craft—Juvenile literature.
Classification: LCC TT872.5 .F45 2024 (print) | LCC TT872.5 (ebook) | DDC 736/.982—dc23/eng/20221209
LC record available at https://lccn.loc.gov/2022051636
LC ebook record available at https://lccn.loc.gov/2022051637

Image Credits
iStockphoto: avean (font), Front Cover, 1, Back Cover; Mighty Media, Inc.: project photos; Shutterstock: Krasowit (ship in bottle), 26, 27, roundex, Front Cover (marble), Sasa-71, Front Cover (seeds), TabitaZn, Back Cover (gift tag), tofang, 6, 7

Design Elements
iStockphoto: Tolga TEZCAN; Shutterstock: ds_vector, Valerii_M

Editorial Credits
Editor: Jessica Rusick
Designers: Aruna Rangarajan, Sarah DeYoung

All internet sites appearing in back matter were available and accurate when this book was sent to press.

The publisher and the author shall not be liable for any damages allegedly arising from the information in this book, and they specifically disclaim any liability from the use or application of any of the contents of this book.

Printed in the United States   5858

TABLE OF CONTENTS

Mini Origami 4

Common Origami Folds 6

Mini Butterflies 8

Mini Throwing Star 10

Mini Fish 12

Mini Paper Airplane 14

Mini Diamonds 16

Mini Potted Plant 20

Mini Boat 24

Mini Crown 28

Read More 32

Internet Sites 32

About the Authors 32

MINI ORIGAMI

Folding figures out of paper is a fun, creative way to pass the time. But what if your paper creations were folded in miniature? Craft itty-bitty, elegant origami artwork to brighten your space or simply to relax!

Fold **tiny fish** to swim in a paper sea.

Craft a **pint-sized crown** fit for a frog prince.

Make **a petite potted plant** to decorate your desk.

Whatever you create, these mini origami projects will be a delight to **FOLD** with **FLAIR!**

BASIC SUPPLIES

» art supplies and glue (optional)
» origami or printer paper
» ruler
» scissors

These miniature projects use paper that is cut smaller than standard origami or printer paper. If you have trouble with a project, try cutting a sheet of paper ½ inch (1.3 cm) longer on each side.

Getting Started

Origami is the Japanese art of paper folding. The art form has been around for centuries. It was originally used in religious ceremonies, but it eventually became a common leisure activity. Traditionally, origami models are based on objects found in nature. But today, people craft all kinds of figures out of paper.

FOLDING GUIDE

Use these markings to guide you as you fold your mini masterpieces. Directions for common folds are found on pages 6 and 7.

- Fold
- Fold and Unfold
- Flip Over
- Direction
- Inside Reverse Fold
- Squash Fold
- Rotate
- Valley Fold
- Crease Line
- Mountain Fold

COMMON ORIGAMI FOLDS

Practice these origami folding techniques to help you with the projects in this book!

VALLEY FOLD
Any fold that creates a trench is a valley fold. Fold the paper's bottom point up so it meets the top point.

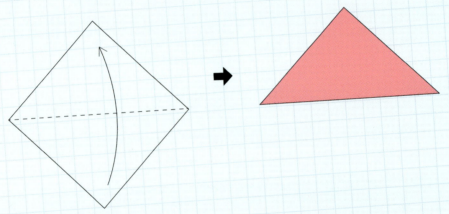

MOUNTAIN FOLD
Any fold that creates a ridge is a mountain fold. Fold the paper's top point behind to meet the bottom point.

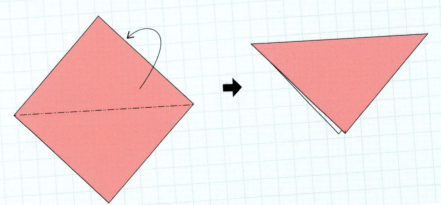

SQUASH FOLD

Squash folds are formed by lifting a pocket and flattening its spine.

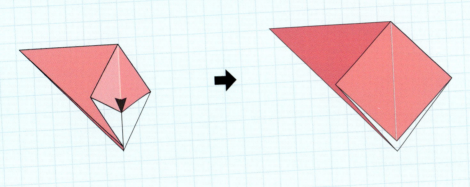

INSIDE REVERSE FOLD

Make an inside reverse fold by pushing an existing crease inward so the folded section is tucked inside the piece.

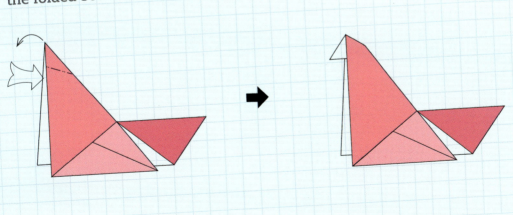

Mini BUTTERFLIES

Build a group of itty-bitty butterflies!

1

Cut a paper square that is 1½ by 1½ inches (4 by 4 centimeters). The facedown side will be the butterfly's color.

2

Valley fold the paper in half horizontally. Valley fold the paper in half vertically. Unfold.

3

Valley fold the top right corner to the bottom left corner and unfold. Valley fold the top left corner to the bottom right corner and unfold.

4

Squash fold the left and right sides. Press the piece down from the top to make a triangle.

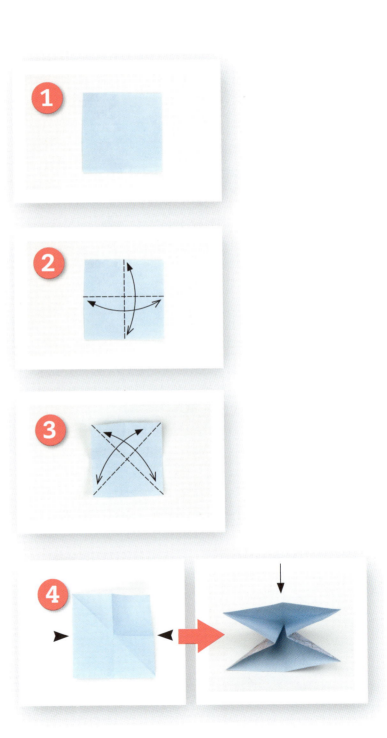

5

Valley fold the bottom right corner up and slightly to the right. Valley fold the bottom left corner up and slightly to the left. Flip the piece over so the top point faces down.

6

Valley fold the bottom point up so it reaches above the paper line. Flip the piece over.

7

Valley fold the tiny triangle down.

8

Push the top of the piece in to crease the center of the triangle. Gently open the top wings of the butterfly.

9

Repeat steps 1 through 8 to create a colorful butterfly brigade.

Mini THROWING STAR

Intertwine colorful bits of paper to create a cool throwing star!

1

Cut two 3-by-3-inch (7.6-by-7.6-cm) paper squares in different colors. Keep one piece on the left and one on the right. Valley fold both pieces in half from the top down. Valley fold both pieces in half again from the top down.

2

Valley fold both pieces in half from left to right and unfold.

3

Valley fold the left side of the left piece upward so its edge aligns with the crease. Valley fold the left side of the right piece downward so its edge aligns with the crease.

4

Valley fold the right side of the left piece down along the crease. Valley fold the right side of the right piece up along the crease. Flip both pieces.

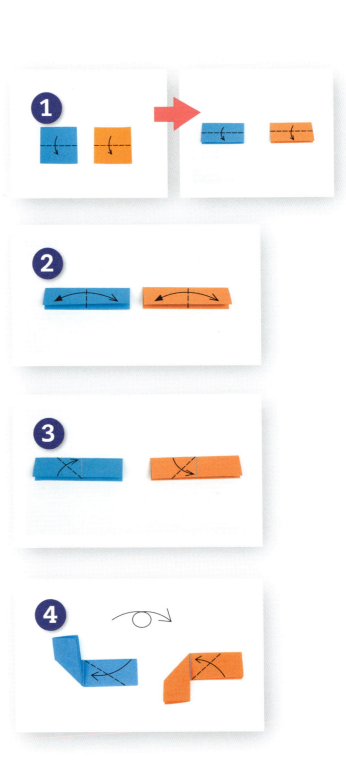

5

Arrange the pieces so the center sections are vertical and parallel. There should be a diamond shape at the top and bottom of each piece. Valley fold the top half of each top diamond down. Valley fold the bottom half of each bottom diamond up.

6

Flip the right piece over and turn it sideways. It will look like two triangles. Set it on top of the left piece.

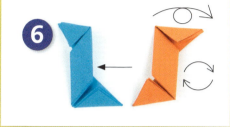

7

Valley fold the top left corner of the bottom piece between the triangles, tucking it under the righthand triangle.

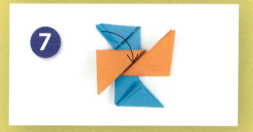

8

Valley fold the bottom right corner beneath the lefthand triangle and tuck it under. Flip the entire piece over.

9

Valley fold the top left corner into the bottom triangle. Valley fold the bottom right corner into the top triangle. Your throwing star is complete!

Mini FISH

Fold a super-small school of colorful fish!

1

Cut a 1½-by-1½-inch (4-by-4-cm) paper square. The side facing up will be the color of the fish. Valley fold the paper in half horizontally. Unfold.

2

Valley fold the paper in half vertically. Unfold.

3

Valley fold the top right corner down to the center of the square. Valley fold the bottom right corner up to the center of the square.

4

Mountain fold the top left corner to the center of the back of the paper. Mountain fold the bottom left corner to the back of the paper.

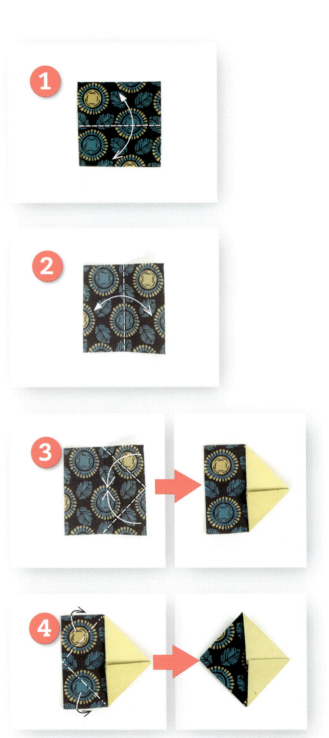

5

Flip the paper over. Valley fold the top point down to the center of the square. Let the triangle on the backside of the paper pop open as you fold. Valley fold the bottom point into the center too. Let the triangle on the backside pop out.

6

Valley fold the point on the left side to the center.

7

Flip the paper over. Your fish is complete! Repeat steps 1 through 6 to create a school of itty-bitty fish. Glue a googly eye on each fish if you'd like!

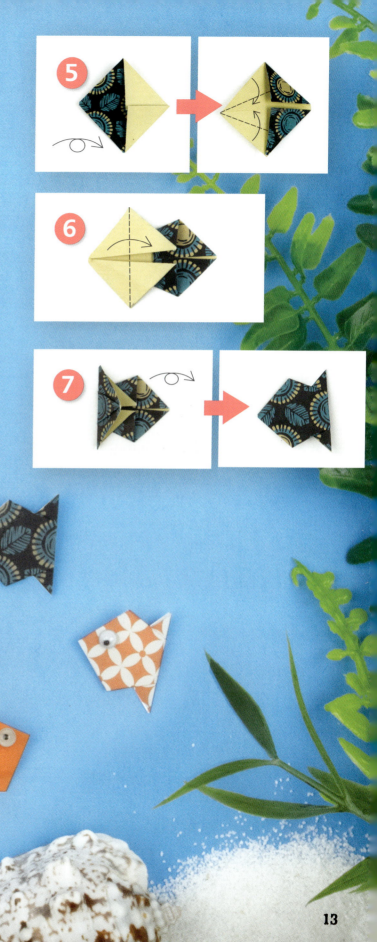

Mini PAPER AIRPLANE

Send your origami flying with this not-so-jumbo jet.

1

Cut a 2½-by-3¼-inch (6-by-8-cm) paper rectangle. Lay it horizontally and valley fold it in half widthwise. Unfold. Then valley fold the top corners down to the center crease.

2

Valley fold the bottom corners up to the edges formed in step 1.

3

Valley fold the bottom section up to form a triangle.

4

Valley fold both bottom corners up to the top point. This will make a diamond shape. Flip the paper over.

5

Valley fold the left and right points to the center.

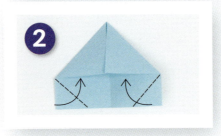
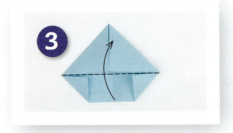

6

Valley fold the diamond in half so the folded points from step 5 are pressed against each other. This will make a trapezoid shape. Rotate the piece 90 degrees clockwise.

7

Valley fold the trapezoid's top layer up so it sticks out at an angle, forming a wing. Turn the trapezoid over and repeat on the other side.

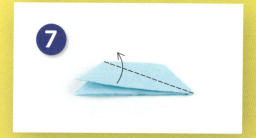

8

Inside reverse fold the pointed piece at the back of the plane so it becomes a tail.

9

Push the sides down so the wings stick out. Your mini airplane is ready to fly!

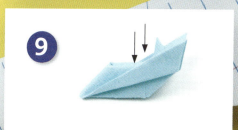

Mini DIAMONDS

Turn folds into facets and make dainty 3D diamonds!

1

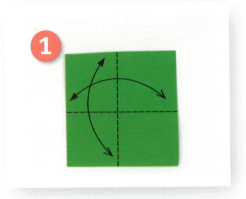

Cut a 2-by-2-inch (5-by-5-cm) paper square. Valley fold the paper in half horizontally and then vertically. Unfold.

2

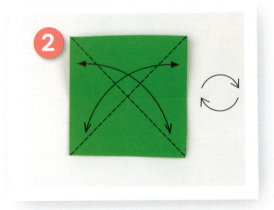

Valley fold the paper diagonally from the top left corner to the bottom right corner. Unfold. Valley fold the paper diagonally from the top right corner to the bottom left corner. Unfold. Then rotate the paper so it looks like a diamond.

3

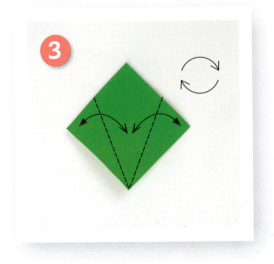

Valley fold the left and right corners in to create a kite shape. Unfold. Rotate the paper 90 degrees clockwise.

4

Repeat step 3 three times so you will have folded and unfolded a kite shape four times total. Rotate the paper so it is a square.

5

Push the right and left edges in toward each other. Press down on the top of the paper to make a trapezoid shape.

6

Crease the trapezoid's edges. Unfold the trapezoid and rotate the paper 90 degrees.

7

Repeat steps 5 through 6.

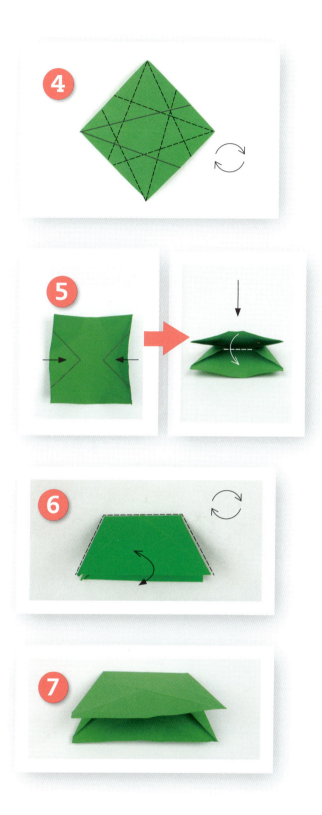

CONTINUED ON THE NEXT PAGE »

8

The creases from steps 5 through 7 will have created a four-pointed star shape. Push the points together to create a diamond shape.

9

Glue the diamond together where its walls meet. Hold the diamond in shape with light pressure as the glue dries.

10

Repeat steps 1 through 9 to make more diamonds. Brush a thin layer of glitter paint on them if you'd like. Then set your diamonds out to sparkle!

Mini POTTED PLANT

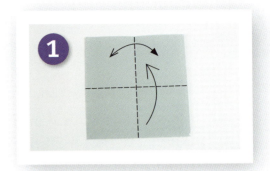

Use decorative paper to craft a cute miniature pot. Fill it with bright green leaves for a perfectly tiny potted plant!

1

Cut a 3-by-3-inch (7.6-by-7.6-cm) paper square. The facedown side will be the color of the pot. Valley fold the square in half from side to side and unfold. Valley fold it in half from bottom to top. This creates a rectangle with a crease down the middle.

2

Valley fold the bottom right corner up to the center crease. Flip the piece over horizontally.

3

Repeat step 2. This will create a triangle. Rotate the triangle 180 degrees.

4

The triangle's bottom will have a center and folded pieces on either side. Open the center. Bring the left corner to meet the right corner. Flatten the piece to create a square.

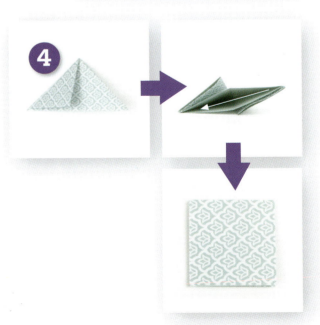

20

5

Rotate the square so it is a diamond with a vertical center crease and a folded point at the bottom that you can't open. Valley fold the point of the top left layer to the crease at an angle. Repeat on the right side. Only the points of the layers should touch. Flip the piece over.

6

Repeat the folds from step 5.

7

Valley fold the top layer of the top point down. Flip the piece over and repeat.

8

Push the two sides of the top layer together. Push the remaining two edges together. Then rotate the piece so it lays flat.

9

Valley fold the top point down. Flip the piece over and repeat.

10

Valley fold the bottom point up. Unfold. Flip the piece over and repeat. Unfold.

CONTINUED ON THE NEXT PAGE »

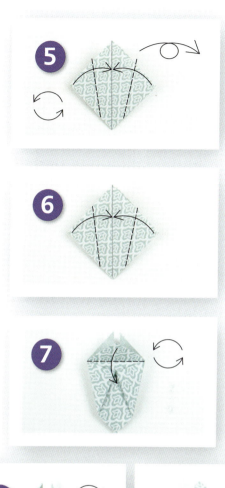
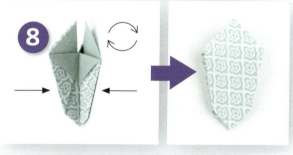

11

Open the wide end of the piece. Flatten the bottom so the piece can stand. This is the pot!

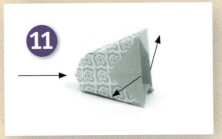

12

Cut a 2-by-2-inch (5-by-5-cm) green paper square. Valley fold the square in half diagonally. Unfold. Rotate the piece so the crease is horizontal.

13

Valley fold the bottom right side up so its edge lines up with the crease. Unfold.

14

Valley fold the bottom right side up again to the crease formed in step 13.

15

Valley fold the top right side down so it lines up with the edge formed in step 14.

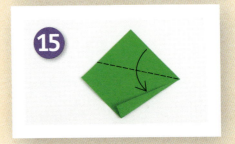

16

Valley fold the skinnier fold up. Valley fold it again so there is a line going almost straight across the length of the piece.

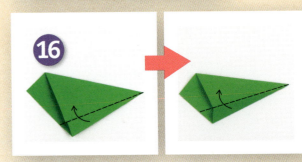

17

Valley fold the wide pointed end over. This creates a leaf with a flat bottom and a pointed top.

18

Repeat steps 12 through 17 to make more leaves. Arrange them in your pot to create a potted plant!

Mini BOAT

This bitty boat is perfect for a relaxing day rowing across a paper pond.

1

Cut a 2½-by-3¼-inch (6-by-8-cm) paper rectangle. Lay it vertically and valley fold it in half from bottom to top.

2

Valley fold the piece in half from side to side and unfold to create a crease.

3

Valley fold both bottom corners up to the center crease. Then rotate the piece 180 degrees.

4

Valley fold the top layer of the bottom flap up so it meets the triangle. Flip the piece over.

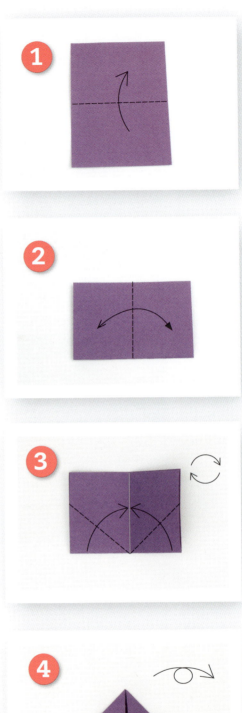

24

5

Valley fold the bottom flap up and unfold.

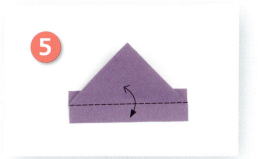

6

Valley fold the bottom corners up to meet the crease.

7

Valley fold the flap back up.

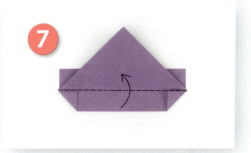

8

Open the bottom of the piece. Pull the sides apart and flatten the piece into a diamond shape. Flip the diamond.

CONTINUED ON THE NEXT PAGE »

25

9

Tuck the unfolded flap at the bottom of the diamond beneath the folded flap.

10

Valley fold the top flap at the bottom of the diamond up. Flip the piece over.

11

Valley fold the bottom of the diamond up. This will make a triangle.

12

Open the bottom of the piece. Push the sides together. Rotate the piece 90 degrees and flatten it into a diamond shape.

13

Pull apart the two sides of the diamond from the top until you have made a boat shape.

14

Adjust the triangle in the middle if needed so it stands straight. Your boat is ready to set sail!

Mini CROWN

Craft a royal headpiece for a tiny king or queen!

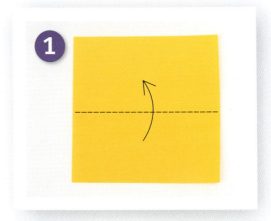

1

Cut a 3-by-3-inch (7.6-by-7.6-cm) paper square. Valley fold it in half from bottom to top to create a rectangle.

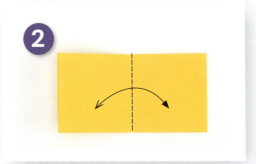

2

Valley fold the rectangle in half from side to side. Unfold.

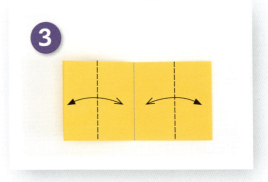

3

Valley fold the sides of the rectangle in to the center crease and unfold halfway.

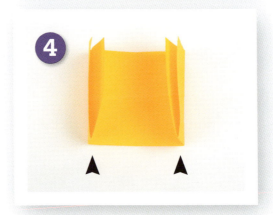

4

Squash fold the sides so that each side has a triangle on the bottom and an open flap on top.

5

Mountain fold the sides of the piece to create a square.

6

Valley fold the top layer of the square's top half down and flip the piece over.

7

Valley fold the top half down to create a rectangle. Rotate the piece 180 degrees.

8

Valley fold the top corners of the top layer down so the sides align with the bottom and center of the rectangle. Unfold the corners halfway.

9

Squash fold the corners you folded in step 8.

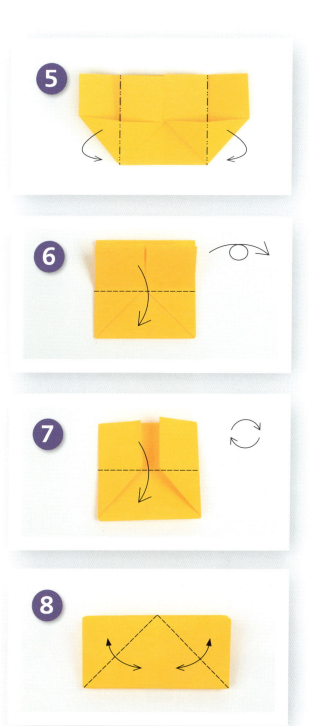

CONTINUED ON THE NEXT PAGE »

10

Lift the bottom edges of the squash folds to reveal two creases that form a center triangle. Mountain fold those creases. As you do, inside reverse fold the bottom edges of the squash folds. This will create a triangle on either side of the center triangle.

11

Mountain fold the triangular flaps on either side of the large triangle. Flip the piece over.

12

Repeat steps 8 through 11.

13

Open the bottom of the piece while pressing down on the top to form a crown.

14

Glue gems to the crown if you'd like!

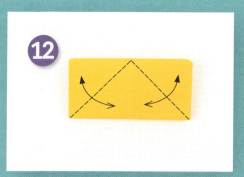

READ MORE

Borgert-Spaniol, Megan. *Mini Projects to Style Your Space*. North Mankato, MN: Capstone Press, 2023.

Harbo, Christopher. *10-Minute Origami Projects*. North Mankato, MN: Capstone Press, 2020.

Sakade, Florence. *Origami Japanese Paper Folding Made Easy: The Perfect Book for Beginners!* North Clarendon, VT: Tuttle Publishing, 2021.

INTERNET SITES

Let's Make Origami!
web-japan.org/kidsweb/virtual/origami/exploring02.html

7 Easy Origami Projects for Kids
www.thesprucecrafts.com/origami-projects-for-kids-4142802

33 Easy & Fun Paper Crafts for Kids
tinybeans.com/perfect-paper-crafts-for-kids/

ABOUT THE AUTHORS

Rebecca Felix is an author and editor of children's books. She loves brainstorming crafts, taking hikes, camping, and learning about all kinds of topics! She collects houseplants in her Minnesota home, where she lives with her funny husband, joyful daughter, and sleepy dog.

Ruthie Van Oosbree is a writer and editor who loves making crafts. In her free time, she enjoys doing word puzzles, reading, and playing the piano. She lives with her husband and three cats in the Twin Cities.